Perspectives

Planet Ocean
How Important is It?

Series Consultant: Linda Hoyt

Flying Start
to Literacy®

Contents

Introduction

How important is the ocean to life on our planet?

The ocean is an amazing place. It covers 70 per cent of our planet. It's an important source of food, not only for the animals that live in the ocean, but for people, too. Billions of people rely on fish and other sea animals and plants for food.

And yet the ocean holds many secrets. Large areas are still unexplored.

Do you think the ocean is important? If so, why?

The big blue ocean

You've probably heard of the Pacific Ocean or the Indian Ocean. But did you know there's really only one ocean? What do you think this means?

The five main oceans have been named.

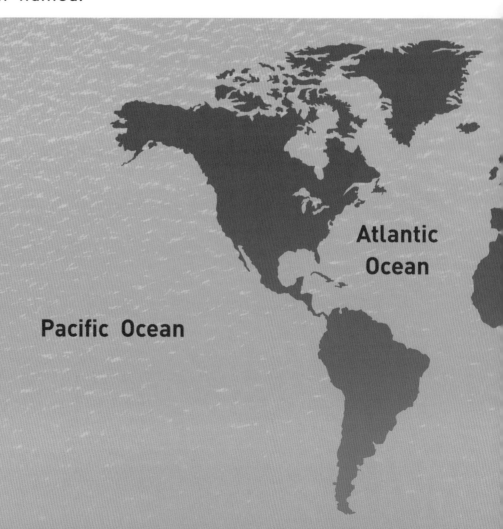

Atlantic Ocean

Pacific Ocean

All of the ocean water on Earth is connected.

And this one ocean is big . . . very big! It covers about 360 million square kilometres – that's about the same size as 47 Australias. And the water in the ocean makes up 97 per cent of all the water on Earth.

What we know about the ocean is amazing. But, what we don't know might amaze you even more!

It is estimated that about 95 per cent of the ocean has not been explored.

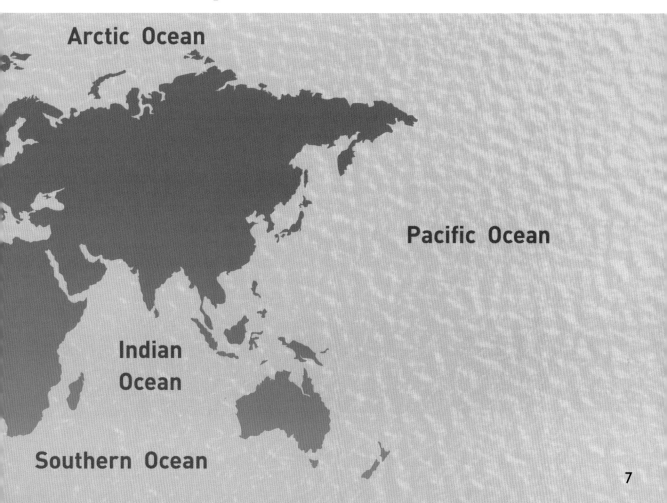

Arctic Ocean

Pacific Ocean

Indian
Ocean

Southern Ocean

Ocean facts

If you could travel down to the ocean floor, it might surprise you to see that it is similar to the earth's surface. It has mountains, canyons and cliffs.

How important do you think it is to know about the ocean?

Tallest

You might think the world's tallest mountain is Mount Everest. But no. The world's tallest mountain rises from the ocean floor. Mauna Kea on Hawaii is about 1,150 metres taller than Mount Everest.

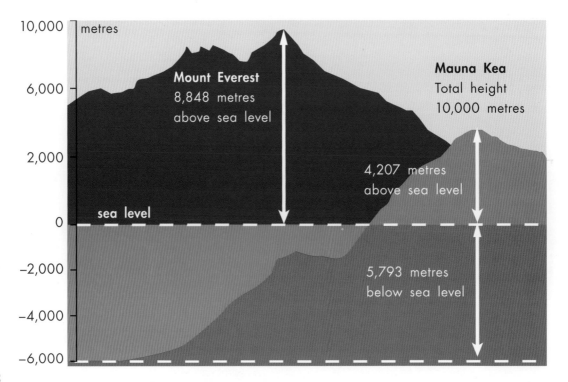

Longest

On land, the Andes in South America is the longest mountain chain. It's more than 6,500 kilometres long. In the ocean, there is a mountain chain that's ten times longer than the Andes. The Mid Ocean Ridge is 65,000 kilometres long.

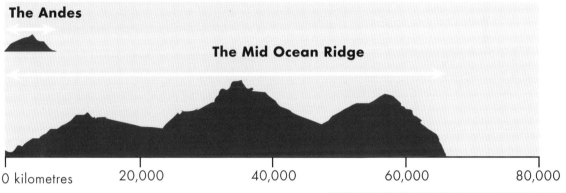

The Andes

The Mid Ocean Ridge

0 kilometres   20,000   40,000   60,000   80,000

Deepest

And where's the world's deepest canyon? You guessed it . . . under the ocean! The Challenger Deep is 11,000 metres below the surface of the ocean. It's six times deeper than the Grand Canyon!

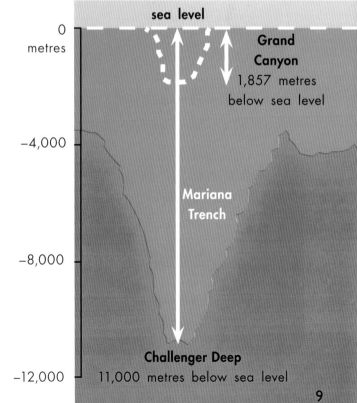

sea level

0 metres

Grand Canyon
1,857 metres below sea level

−4,000

Mariana Trench

−8,000

Challenger Deep
11,000 metres below sea level

−12,000

9

Speak out!

Read what these students think about the ocean.

The ocean provides food for many species. Fish provide food for many living things, such as polar bears, sharks, whales and people. Without the ocean, we wouldn't have enough to eat.

Many lives have been saved because of the ocean's waters. Firefighters collect huge amounts of ocean water in special helicopters to dump on bushfires.

Ocean tourism makes money through cruises, diving and whale watching. Touring the coastal and ocean environment is an unforgettable experience.

More animals live in the ocean than on land. If these ocean animals lose their homes through pollution, for example, it wouldn't just affect life in the ocean. It would affect us. The ocean is part of the circle of life.

Stop overfishing!

Every day, we take a quarter of a billion kilograms of seafood out of the ocean to eat. Look at what has happened to the number of Pacific Ocean sardines.

What does this mean for the sea animals that need sardines to survive?

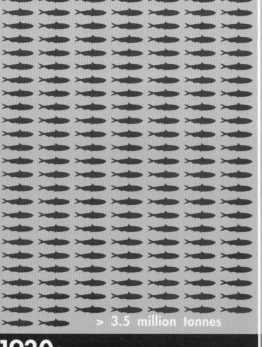

> 3.5 million tonnes

1930s

100,000 tonnes

2015

Ocean animals depend on a healthy sardine population

Since 2010, the number of newborn pelicans has dropped because of a lack of prey, including sardines.

Californian sea lion pups eat sardines. The drop in the number of sardines means many sea pups starve.

Sailfish and whales are just two of the many animals in the sea that regularly eat sardines. Fewer sardines means that larger animals like sailfish and whales have to find other fish to eat.

Planet Ocean?

Some people say that it is wrong to call our planet Earth when it is mostly ocean.

What do you think?

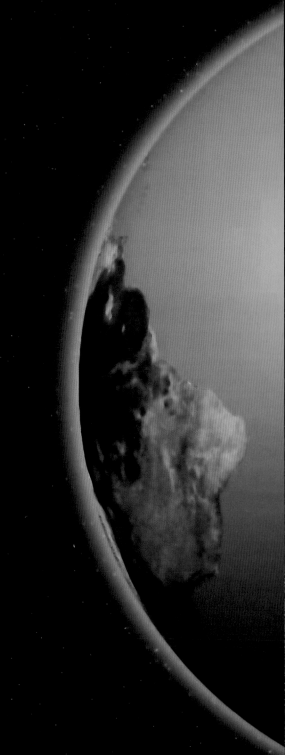

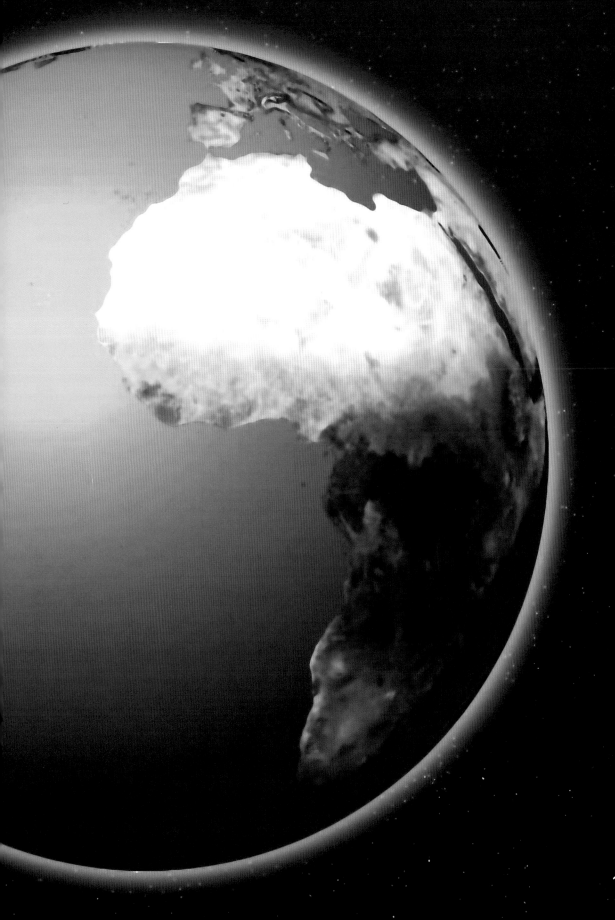

How to write about your opinion

State your opinion

Think about the main question in the introduction on page 4 of this book. What is your opinion?

Research

Look for other information that you need to back up your opinion.

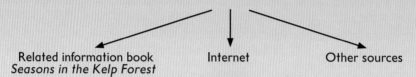

| Related information book *Seasons in the Kelp Forest* | Internet | Other sources |

Make a plan

Introduction

How will you "hook" the reader to get them interested?

Write a sentence that makes your opinion clear.

List reasons to support your opinion.

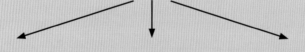

| Support your reason with examples. | Support your reason with examples. | Support your reason with examples. |

Conclusion

Write a sentence that makes your opinion clear. Leave your reader with a strong message.

Publish

Publish your writing.

Include some graphics or visual images.